DEPRESSION
Walking from Darkness into the Dawn

JUNE HUNT

Depression: Walking from Darkness into the Dawn
Copyright © 2013 Hope For The Heart
Aspire Press is an imprint of
Hendrickson Publishers Marketing, LLC
P.O. Box 3473
Peabody, Massachusetts 01961-3473 USA
www.hendricksonrose.com

All Scripture quotations, unless otherwise indicated, are taken from the Holy Bible, New International Version® NIV®. Copyright © 1973, 1978, 1984, International Bible Society. Used by permission of Zondervan. All rights reserved worldwide.

The views and opinions expressed in this book are those of the author(s) and do not necessarily express the views of Hendrickson Publishers, nor is this book intended to be a substitute for mental health treatment or professional counseling.

The information in this resource is intended as guidelines for healthy living. Please consult qualified medical, legal, pastoral, and psychological professionals regarding individual concerns.

For more information on Hope For The Heart, visit www.hopefortheheart.org or call 1-800-488-HOPE (4673).

Printed in the United States of America

September 2017, 12th printing

CONTENTS

ear friend,

Do you feel the weight of the world on your shoulders? Do you feel stuck in a painful situation—you can't see the light at the end of the tunnel? Do you say to yourself, "I can't *see* anything that's good. I can't *feel* any sense of happiness. I can't will myself out of feeling so down!" If so, like millions of people, you are under the dark clouds of depression. And, if so, *I truly understand!*

When I was a teenager, I felt deeply depressed over the pain in my family. My father was not only unfaithful to my mother, but also verbally and emotionally abusive toward everyone in our family.

Struggling in the darkness of depression, I looked at life through a black filter. I had difficulty seeing any good in my circumstances and certainly couldn't see anything good in myself. I harbored hatred in my heart, felt helpless in the "here-and-now" and hopeless about the future. The pain was so intense, I even wondered if I was going crazy.

Then one day I genuinely invited Jesus into my heart and gave Him control of my life. The hurt in my heart didn't go away, but the Lord lifted the excessive burden that was crushing my spirit.

Today I can truly say,

> *"Praise be to the LORD, to God our Savior,*
> *who daily bears our burdens."*
> (Psalm 68:19)

If you are walking in the darkness of depression, I hope these truths that made the real difference in my life will be helpful to you.

#1 You need to see your life from God's perspective. He cares about you and has positive plans for your life. The Lord says, *"For I know the plans I have for you … plans to prosper you and not to harm you, plans to give you hope and a future"* (Jeremiah 29:11).

#2 You need to know that God has a purpose for everything that touches you. Nothing in your life occurs that has not first been filtered through God's fingers of love. If God permits it, He guarantees He will use it for your good and for His glory. Romans 8:28 says, *"We know that in all things God works for the good of those who love him, who have been called according to his purpose."*

#3 You need to know that there will be times when your heart will be pressed down, but also times of restoration because God is a healer of broken hearts. He heals us when we give our heart to Him. And, He knows how to restore our joy. Second Corinthians 4:8–9 says, *"We are hard pressed on every side, but not crushed; perplexed, but not in despair; persecuted, but not abandoned; struck down, but not destroyed."*

#4 You need to know that no matter how great your despondency, God can open your eyes to His unique design for your life. Just as storms replenish the dry, parched soil, giving birth to new life, the storms in your life can revitalize your relationship with the Lord and give birth to personal growth beyond what you could ever imagine. Psalm 119:67 says, *"Before I was afflicted I went astray, but now I obey your word."*

If you are struggling with depression, my prayer is that you will see this time as an opportunity to allow the light of God's love to comfort you, carry you and encourage you so that you can walk from the darkness into the dawn.

Yours in the Lord's hope,

June

June Hunt

"The Lord is my light and my salvation—whom shall I fear? The Lord is the stronghold of my life—of whom shall I be afraid?"
(Psalm 27:1)

DEPRESSION
Walking from Darkness into the Dawn

On June 20, 2001, the entire city—the nation, the world—was stunned when Andrea Yates systematically drowned her children in the bathtub—all five of her children ranging in age from six months to seven years.[1]

In rapid fire, the shocked world asked, *How could a mother do the unthinkable—kill her own children? What could drive a mother to commit such a heinous crime, five times in a row?* In a word, the answer is *depression*—but not just "normal depression," rather a *psychotic depression* that caused Andrea to break with reality.[2] Couldn't someone have rescued this mother and these innocent children from their ultimate doom? The simple answer is *yes*. And the Lord admonishes us all to …

"Rescue those being led away to death; hold back those staggering toward slaughter. If you say, 'But we knew nothing about this,' does not he who weighs the heart perceive it?
Does not he who guards your life know it? Will he not repay each person according to what he has done?"
(Proverbs 24:11–12)

DEFINITIONS OF DEPRESSION

Have the dark clouds of depression poured their tears upon your soul?

Do you feel stuck in your situation, muddled in your mind, mired in your emotions?

Creative geniuses and slow learners alike, international leaders and migrant farmers have struggled beneath the black clouds of depression. Can anything bring back the blue skies of contentment in the midst of depression?

King David of Israel discovered the answer to this question—he exchanged the darkness of despair for the light of God's hope:

"Why are you downcast, O my soul?
Why so disturbed within me?
Put your hope in God, for I will yet praise
him, my Savior and my God."
(Psalm 42:11)

If you place a heavy iron on a heart-shaped pillow, the buoyant pillow becomes pressed down—"depressed." But the next day, if you remove the iron, the pillow pops right back to its original form. However, if you wait to remove the iron for months, the pillow will not spring back to its original shape. Instead, the pillow will be flat and stay depressed. A pillow, which can sustain temporary pressure, is not designed to hold its shape for long under heavy pressure.

The same is true for the human heart. When it is "pressed down" due to normal pressure from normal situations (situational depression), your heart is made by God to be capable of rebounding once the pressure is removed. However, He did not design you to live under the weight of heavy pressure for long periods of time without having your heart enter into a "state" of depression. During those painful times when *hope seems* elusive, your emotions feel flat and your heart feels sick, Solomon, the wise author of the book of Proverbs, explains that *"Hope deferred makes the heart sick."* (Proverbs 13:12)

▶ Depression is literally a condition of being "pressed down" to a lower position (as in a footprint).[3]

▶ Depression can refer to a state of decline and reduced activity (as in an economic depression).[4]

▶ The apostle Paul used the Greek word **bareo**, which means "pressed or weighed down" to describe the immense emotional pressure and severe hardships that he and Timothy suffered at the hands of those who opposed Christ.[5]

**"We do not want you
to be uninformed, brothers,
about the hardships we suffered
in the province of Asia.
We were under great pressure,
far beyond our ability to endure,
so that we despaired even of life.
Indeed, in our hearts
we felt the sentence of death."
(2 Corinthians 1:8–9)**

In ancient writings, the earliest reference for our word *depression* was the word *melancholia* (literally "black bile"). The assumption was that the melancholy person had an excess of black bile, which resulted in depression.

In the second century AD, a physician named Aretaeus referred to his melancholy patients as "sad, dismayed, sleepless. They become thin by their agitation and loss of refreshing sleep. At a more advanced state, they complain of a thousand futilities and desire death."[6]

Even today *melancholia* is defined as "a mental condition characterized by extreme depression, bodily complaints, and often hallucinations and delusions."[7]

Psychological depression is a state in which the heart is pressed down and unable to experience joy. Those suffering with depression feel trapped underneath a pervasive canopy of sadness, grief, guilt and hopelessness.

Psychology is the science or study of the mind as it relates to thoughts, feelings and behaviors, focusing on why people think, feel and act as they do.[8] Thus, the term psychological depression pertains to the mental, emotional and behavioral characteristics of a depressed person.

Psychological depression is a condition that impacts the whole person: body (the physical), soul (the mind, the will, and the emotions) and spirit (the source of our deepest inner needs).

Psychological depression is an umbrella term that covers feelings from mild discouragement to intense despair.[9]

How we respond to our hurts and losses in life is all important. Jesus cares about our hearts and knows that we are especially vulnerable when we are heavy hearted. He cautions us…

> **"Be careful, or your hearts**
> **will be weighed down**
> **with dissipation, drunkenness**
> **and the anxieties of life,**
> **and that day will close on you**
> **unexpectedly like a trap."**
> **(Luke 21:34)**

1 *Normal* depression—situational or reactive depression

- An *involuntary* reaction to painful pressure

- The *normal problems* of life press down the heart for a short period of time (rejection, failure, illness).

- The *transitional stages* of life often press the heart down (adolescence, empty nest, midlife crises, major moves, menopause, retirement).

2 *Masked* depression—hidden depression

- A state of ***buried*** unresolved conflict

- True painful feelings are denied or covered up.

- Relief from pain is unconsciously found in self-effort or excessive activity.

3 *Neurotic* depression—a minor Depressive Disorder[10]

- A ***prolonged*** state of depression (longer than the normal time frame needed for emotional recovery)

- The symptoms interfere with normal biological and social activities.

- The cause can usually be traced to a precipitating event.

4 *Psychotic* depression—a major Depressive Disorder[11]

- A ***severe*** state of depression

- A psychosis involves dissociation or a loss of contact with reality.

- The psychotic person can experience hallucinations, delusions and/or schizophrenia.

Every year, new maladies as well as new medicines come on the scene. So, how "new" is depression? As far back as the fourth century BC the famous physician Hippocrates gave the first clinical description of melancholia, including the erratic mood swings of what today is called Bipolar Disorder. And even over 500 years earlier, the psalmist King David gave this vivid description of his emotions during one of the most severe storms in his life.

> "My thoughts trouble me
> and I am distraught. ...
> My heart is in anguish within me;
> the terrors of death assail me.
> Fear and trembling have beset me;
> horror has overwhelmed me.
> I said, 'Oh, that I had the wings
> of a dove! I would fly away and
> be at rest—I would flee far away
> and stay in the desert;
> I would hurry to my place of shelter,
> far from the tempest and storm.'"
> (Psalm 55:2, 4–8)

1 *Depressive* disorders: Unipolar depression

- Unipolar (*uni* = one, *polar* = pole) refers to "one extreme end."

- Unipolar is characterized by one extreme, emotionally low state.

- Unipolar is the most common type of depression.

2 *Bipolar* disorders—formerly called manic-depression

- Bipolar (*bi* = two, *polar* = pole) refers to "two opposite ends."

- Bipolar is characterized by an alternating pattern of extreme emotional highs and lows called mania and depression.

- Episodes of mania are characterized by traits such as increased activity, incessant talking, loss of appetite/sleep and often excessive spending, grandiose thinking, poor judgment, immorality, impulsive behavior, hostile aggression and suicidal thinking.

3 *Etiological* disorders—literally, disorders based on etiology.[12]

- *Etiology* means "cause" or "origin."[13]

- Under this classification are two primary types.

The first type of etiological depression is the Mood Disorder Due to a General Medical Condition. This means that the *unhealthy* changes in the body due to illness cause psychological depression. For example, 25–40 percent of those with a neurological condition (Parkinson's, Huntington's and Alzheimer's diseases, Multiple Sclerosis and stroke) develop a marked depression during illness.

The second type of etiological depression is Substance-Induced Mood Disorder. This means that something entering the body causes depression. The substance could be medication, drugs or exposure to a toxin (examples: alcohol, sedatives, birth control pills, medications to treat various diseases such as Parkinson's).

QUESTION: "Is depression a sin?"

ANSWER: Not always, but it can become sin when …[14]

▶ You are depressed over the consequences of your sinful actions, and you don't attempt to change.

▶ You are depressed because you choose to let others control you instead of choosing to obey Christ and allowing Him to be in control.

▶ You use depression to manipulate others.

▶ You don't take the necessary steps for healing (seeking help and biblical counseling, memorizing Scriptures, reading Christian materials).

▶ You hold on to self-pity and anger.

▶ You continually choose to blame God and others for your unhappiness.

Biblical Example: Book of Jonah

Jonah's depression is an example of reactive depression as a result of sin. Jonah is a man called by God. Yet he ends up angry, pouting and in the depths of depression. How does Jonah become so deeply depressed?

Chapter 1: *Disobedience*

Jonah is called by the Lord to preach God's truth to the godless people of Nineveh. But Jonah rebels and boards a ship going in a different direction. When Jonah's disobedience brings repercussions on the ship's crew, he is rejected and literally thrown overboard.

Chapter 2: *Dread*

Recognizing that the judgment of God is upon him to the point of losing his life (inside the belly of a great fish), Jonah cries out for mercy. The Lord extends mercy and spares his life.

Chapter 3: *Declaration*

Jonah resigns himself to obey God's call. He declares God's truth, and all the godless people repent.

Chapter 4: *Depression*

Jonah becomes angry with God for extending mercy to those whom Jonah doesn't deem worthy of mercy. Ultimately, Jonah plunges into a severe depression in which he is consumed with bitterness, self-pity and despair to the extent of wanting to die. Jonah even states, *"I am angry enough to die."* (Jonah 4:9)

CHARACTERISTICS OF DEPRESSION

Were there any clues to the seriousness of Andrea Yates' mental depression? Did anyone realize the children could be in serious danger? After the five children were drowned by their mother, the media quickly learned that this rigidly religious family had been dealing with Andrea's severe depression for several years. The newspapers reported that in 1999 she had attempted suicide twice. And because of her severe postpartum depression, following the birth of their fourth son, the couple was also advised to have no more children—yet a fifth child was born.

The Yates' situation is certainly not the norm and, although many people become seriously despondent, the majority of those who experience common depression will never be led to commit acts that result in such drastic consequences. Yet because all types of depression carry a heavy sense of hopelessness, what can we do when life becomes weary and meaningless? Who can we count on to renew our strength and our hope in the future?

The Bible says, *"[The Lord] will not grow tired or weary, and his understanding no one can fathom. He gives strength to the weary and increases the power of the weak. Even youths grow tired and weary, and young men stumble and fall; but those who hope in the Lord will renew their strength. They will soar on wings like eagles; they will run and not grow weary, they will walk and not be faint."* (Isaiah 40:28–31)

WHAT SYMPTOMS Characterize the Four Types of Depression?

We all experience normal depression or "the blues" from time to time when life doesn't go as planned or physical exhaustion leaves us drained of our natural ability to rebound from disappointments. During these times, we can mask our real feelings from ourselves, closing off authentic intimacy with the Lord and others. However, failure to honestly confront our feelings can lead to clinical depression (neurotic or psychotic depression). But those who heed the danger signs and work through their painful feelings—although it may take weeks and months—will avoid needless and excessive suffering.

"A prudent man sees danger and takes refuge, but the simple keep going and suffer for it." (Proverbs 22:3)

Classic Characteristics of Depression

MIND	
Normal Depression • self-doubt • worry/fear • forgetfulness	**Masked Depression** • self-inflation • appearance of invincibility • disorganized thoughts
Neurotic Depression • self-criticism • hypochondria • inability to make decisions	**Psychotic Depression** • self-rejection • hallucinations • lack of judgment or reasoning

EMOTIONS	
Normal Depression • anger • sadness • diminished joy	**Masked Depression** • suppressed anger • distraction • self-sacrifice
Neurotic Depression • anger • hopelessness • no pleasure	**Psychotic Depression** • acute anger • schizophrenia • no pleasure

WILL

Normal Depression	Masked Depression
• irritability • activity pattern upset	• judgmentalism • increased activity
Neurotic Depression • apathy • diminished activity	**Psychotic Depression** • unresponsiveness • catatonia

BODY

Normal Depression	Masked Depression
• loss of appetite • sleep difficulty • no death threat	• weight gain • less need for sleep • hidden death threat
Neurotic Depression • weight loss • escape by sleeping • manipulates with death threat	**Psychotic Depression** • weight loss • severe insomnia • severe death threat

Certain Bible passages might be reflective of these four classic types of depression.

▶ *Normal* **Depression**

> *"Why does your face look so sad when you are not ill? This can be nothing but sadness of heart."* (Nehemiah 2:2)

▶ *Masked* **Depression**

> *"Even in laughter the heart may ache."* (Proverbs 14:13)

▶ *Neurotic* **Depression**

> *"I groan in anguish of heart. … My strength fails me; even the light has gone from my eyes. … I am like a deaf man, who cannot hear, like a mute, who cannot open his mouth; I have become like a man who does not hear, whose mouth can offer no reply."* (Psalm 38:8, 10, 13–14)

▶ *Psychotic* **Depression**

> *"My days vanish like smoke. … My heart is blighted and withered like grass; I forget to eat my food. … I lie awake; I have become like a bird alone on a roof. … I eat ashes as my food and mingle my drink with tears. … I wither away like grass."* (Psalm 102:3–4, 7, 9, 11)

QUESTION: "What are some of the symptoms of postpartum depression and postpartum psychosis?"[15]

ANSWER:

- Excessive concern for the baby's well-being

- A lack of interest in the baby

- Sadness and loss of energy

- Not feeling love for the baby or for her family

- Feeling anger toward her baby and family

- Increase or decrease of appetite

- Anxiety or panic attacks

- Overly critical of her ability to be a good mother

- Fear of harming her baby—if these thoughts are delusional, there may be a risk of harm to the baby

- Voices and/or visions of Satan/demons attacking her ability to be a good mother, encouraging her to destroy her child

Those who struggle in the darkness of depression have difficulty seeing the good in their circumstances and especially in themselves. They look at life through a "black filter." The photographer who uses a black lens can take a picture during the daytime, but the final photograph will appear to be a night scene. Depressed people see life through a black filter, feeling hatred toward themselves, helpless about their situations and hopeless over their future. If you are walking in the darkness of depression, you need to see the light of the Lord and know that He cares.

> **"Look to my right and see; no one is concerned for me. I have no refuge; no one cares for my life. I cry to you, O Lord; I say, 'You are my refuge, my portion in the land of the living.'"**
> **(Psalm 142:4–5)**

What you say about yourself

- "I can't do anything right!"
- "Why try?"
- "My usefulness is over!"
- "I hate myself!"
- "Look at so-and-so (by comparison)."
- "I must have done something wrong!"
- "Nobody loves me!"

What is the light of truth?

The Lord says, *"I have loved you with an everlasting love; I have drawn you with loving-kindness."* (Jeremiah 31:3)

What you say about your situation

- "I don't see any way out!"
- "It didn't matter anyway!"
- "I can't do anything about it!"
- "I can't bear it!"
- "This is intolerable!"
- "It's not fair!"
- "I'm helpless to change it!"

What is the light of truth?

I can say with Paul, *"I can do everything through him who gives me strength."* (Philippians 4:13)

What you say about your future

- "So what!"
- "Nothing will change."
- "It's hopeless!"
- "No one will ever love me!"
- "I'll be too old."
- "That was my last chance for happiness!"
- "I have nothing to live for."

What is the light of truth?

The Lord says, *"'For I know the plans I have for you,' declares the LORD, 'plans to prosper you and not to harm you, plans to give you hope and a future.'"* (Jeremiah 29:11)

If you are walking in darkness, cherish these words from the Lord.

**"I will lead the blind by ways they have not known, along unfamiliar paths I will guide them; I will turn the darkness into light before them and make the rough places smooth.
These are the things I will do;
I will not forsake them."
(Isaiah 42:16)**

Note: If you are experiencing any of these physical problems, be sure to consult your health-care professional.

CAUSES OF DEPRESSION

As for Andrea Yates, she became spiritually unbalanced with a greater focus on Satan and sin than on God and grace. Ultimately, she had visions and heard voices that claimed she was evil. Satan was inside her, and the only way to be rid of him was for her to be executed! "She had to kill the children, as Satan demanded, in order to get the death penalty."

Andrea said about her children, "They stumbled because I was evil. The way I was raising them they could never be saved. They were doomed to perish in the fires of hell."[16] Ultimately, after all five deaths, she hoped that her children would be in heaven.

> **"There is a way that seems right
> to a man, but in the end
> it leads to death."
> (Proverbs 14:12)**

Most people know little about hormonal postpartum depression. Andrea Yates suffered from this disorder long before having her fifth child. While 60–70 percent of birth mothers experience mild depression called *postnatal* or "*baby blues*" (unexplained crying, mood swings and irritability), these symptoms usually abate after a few weeks. However, 5–20 percent experience *postpartum depression*, which is distinguished from the "baby blues" both by its long duration and the debilitating indifference of the mother toward herself and her children.[17]

Andrea Yates had been suicidal, hospitalized and recently taken off the medications that had been helpful to her. Then she was struggling with *postpartum psychosis* (a break with reality). Because of the hormonal fluctuations in the mother's body, this psychotic disorder affects one or two out of every 1,000 birth mothers.[18]

Tragically, many of these mothers with postpartum psychosis are consumed with thoughts of death to their babies and destruction of themselves.

"The cords of death entangled me; the torrents of destruction overwhelmed me. The cords of the grave coiled around me; the snares of death confronted me."
(Psalm 18:4–5)

Six Physical Contributors to Depression

1. Hormonal imbalance
2. Medications and drugs
3. Chronic illnesses
4. Melancholy temperament
5. Improper food, rest, exercise
6. Genetic vulnerability

"Fifty percent of those with bipolar have at least one parent with the disorder."[19] People who have had depressed, close family members are two times more vulnerable to depression.[20]

QUESTION: "Is depression sometimes caused by a chemical imbalance in the brain?"

ANSWER: Yes. For example, hormonal changes during puberty, postpartum (after childbirth) and perimenopause (around menopause) can lead to depression, as can a thyroid deficiency.

QUESTION: "Why do twice as many women have depression as men?"[21]

ANSWER: Women produce only one half the amount of serotonin as men do. However, estrogen in women multiplies the amount of serotonin to equal the level in men. Prior to a woman's menstrual cycle, after childbirth and around menopause, estrogen levels drop, sometimes severely. When a woman's estrogen level is not sufficient to multiply serotonin, she experiences a depletion of serotonin, which can cause depression. This is one reason why many women receive Estrogen Replacement Therapy (ERT).

QUESTION: "What happens to the brain when a person suffers a major depression?"[22]

ANSWER: Medical research verifies that some people have a condition in the brain called hippocampal atrophy, which results from a chemical imbalance (such as too much or too little adrenal cortisol) in the hippocampus region of the brain. During these states of depression the hippocampus physically shrinks.

Some people say, "Depression is *anger turned inward*." That statement is not always true, but it is true when anger is repressed. *Repression* occurs when unacceptable desires and emotions are blocked from a person's awareness and left to operate in the unconscious.[23] This *stuffed anger* or *swallowed anger* takes longer to come into God's light so that any underlying bitterness can be exposed. Bitterness can be a cause of depression. Ezekiel had this kind of bitter anger in his spirit when the Lord sent him for seven days to those who had been exiled.

"I went in bitterness and in the anger of my spirit, with the strong hand of the LORD upon me." (Ezekiel 3:14)

Repressed anger over:

- *loss* of a loved one
- *loss* of control
- *loss* of expectations
- *loss* of health or abilities
- *loss* of self-esteem
- *loss* of possessions
- *loss* of respect for others
- *loss* of personal goals

Suppressed fear of:

- losing a job
- empty nest
- abandonment
- being alone
- dying
- failure
- growing old
- rejection

Internalized stress over:

- new job
- marital problems
- financial obligations
- troubled child
- relocation
- workload
- family responsibilities
- alcoholic spouse

Even our deep disappointments must be resolved or else our bitterness will cause trouble, and unresolved anger and bitterness will hurt those close to us.

"See to it that no one misses the grace of God and that no bitter root grows up to cause trouble and defile many."
(Hebrews 12:15)

Just as there are physical, emotional and mental reasons for depression, there are also spiritual reasons for a despairing heart. Disobedience and guilt provide enough fertile seed to turn any white cloud into a dark storm. You cannot harbor the guilt of displeasing God and still experience the full joy of His salvation. Nor can you withstand the schemes and attacks of the enemy against your mind without knowing and appropriating the Word of Life into your life.

Disobedience and guilt are inseparable. And unless you apply the remedy of confession and repentance (a change of mind and a change of direction), you may find depression sweeping over your soul and spirit and, as did the disobedient Israelites.

**"You will find no repose,
no resting place for the sole of your foot.
There the Lord will give you an anxious
mind, eyes weary with longing,
and a despairing heart."
(Deuteronomy 28:65)**

Elijah's Descent into Depression

(Adaptation of portions of this data used by permission from Larry Crabb, New Way Ministries.)

▶ *Loss*

One or more basic needs are threatened.

- love
- significance
- security

Elijah's security was threatened.

"Elijah was afraid and ran for his life. When he came to Beersheba in Judah, he left his servant there." (1 Kings 19:3)

▶ *Negative Thinking Patterns*

- self-pity
- self-condemnation
- fear
- hopelessness

Elijah thought to himself, *I have had enough*, and asked God to take his life.

"He himself went a day's journey into the desert. He came to a broom tree, sat down under it and prayed that he might die. 'I have had enough, Lord,' he said. 'Take

my life; I am no better than my ancestors.'"
(1 Kings 19:4)

▶ *Repressed Anger*

Buried resentment over circumstances.

Elijah was frustrated that all his efforts seemed in vain.

"He replied, 'I have been very zealous for the LORD God Almighty. The Israelites have rejected your covenant, broken down your altars, and put your prophets to death with the sword. I am the only one left, and now they are trying to kill me too.'"
(1 Kings 19:10)

▶ *Depression*

Elijah turns to God.

WHEN ONE TURNS TO GOD

No Depression

- Admits anger
- Hope in God, personal identity is in Christ
- Acts in power of Christ
- Relies on Christ's Spirit

Masked Depression

- Denies anger
- Hope in God, but no identity in Christ
- Acts on general promises of God
- Relies on self-effort

WHEN ONE DOESN'T TURN TO GOD

Masked Depression

- Admits anger
- Hope in empty replacements
- Acts to replace loss with substitutes
- Relies on false reality

Neurotic Depression

- Denies anger
- Perceives little hope
- Acts out of negative thinking patterns
- Relies on medication and other people

Psychotic Depression

- Denies anger
- Perceives no hope
- Acts to promote self-destruction
- Relies on total escape from reality

ROOT CAUSE of Staying Stuck in Depression

▶ **WRONG BELIEF:**

"The failures, losses and disappointments in my life have robbed me of all joy. There's no hope for my future, and there's nothing I can do about it."

▶ **RIGHT BELIEF:**

"I admit I am depressed over the circumstances in my life. But Christ lives in me, and He is my hope. I will choose to renew my mind with God's truth and do whatever I need to do in order to experience the future He planned for me."

**"In our hearts we felt
the sentence of death.
But this happened that we might
not rely on ourselves but on God,
who raises the dead. ...
On him we have set our hope
that he will continue to deliver us."
(2 Corinthians 1:9–10)**

STEPS TO SOLUTION

Were the family and friends of Andrea Yates aware of the seriousness of her depression?[24] Many people wondered, *Did Andrea's husband do enough to ensure his wife's safety and the safety of their children?*

The court trial revealed that Rusty had admitted Andrea to institutions for her severe depression several times, and twice she was released prematurely. He appealed (unsuccessfully) to her last doctor, stating that she needed the medication that had proved successful in the past. Eventually a schedule was arranged where Rusty left for work every morning at 9:00; then his mother came at 10:00 to help Andrea with the children, their home schooling and the housework. Andrea was left alone at home with the children for only one hour out of each day! But during that one hour on June 20, 2001, Andrea carried out each drowning.

How could this tragedy have been avoided? What steps could loved ones have taken to help Andrea move from the darkness of despair into the light of hope. If they had been aware of the danger, they could have learned much more about this malady and been discerning about what to do.

> **"Let the wise listen
> and add to their learning,
> and let the discerning get guidance."**
> **(Proverbs 1:5)**

TAKE OFF the Masks

As we go through painful events in our lives, we can sweep them under the rug and not acknowledge them or we can choose to see them only in a light we can accept. However, in doing so, we fail to grieve over our hurts and losses. By wearing masks, we try to protect our hearts and hide who we really are and what we don't want to face. But this kind of masquerade blocks our maturity and our ability to have intimacy with God and others. Don't ever fear allowing God to hold your hand and help you see the reality of your pain and how He has been working through the painful experiences in your life.

> **"Surely you desire truth in the inner
> parts; you teach me wisdom in the
> inmost place."**
> **(Psalm 51:6)**

Key Passage to Read and Reread

1 Thessalonians 5:16–24

▶ *"Be joyful always."* (v. 16)

Choose to focus on the positives in your life.

▶ *"Pray continually."* (v. 17)

Choose to talk to God about everything.

▶ *"Give thanks in all circumstances."* (v. 18)

Choose to thank God for what you are learning right now.

▶ *"Do not put out the Spirit's fire."* (v. 19)

Choose to change when God's Spirit convicts you to change.

▶ *"Do not treat prophecies with contempt."* (v. 20)

Choose to take God's Word seriously.

▶ *"Test everything."* (v. 21)

Choose to ask, "Is this right in God's sight?"

▶ *"Hold on to the good."* (v. 21)

Choose to do right, even when tempted to do wrong.

▶ *"Avoid every kind of evil."* (v. 22)

Choose to immediately turn from temptation.

▶ *Realize, God has already sanctified you through and through.* (v. 23)

Choose to see how God has "set you apart" to be what He intended you to be.

▶ *Aim to keep your whole spirit, soul and body blameless.* (v. 23)

Choose to commit your whole being to doing what God created you to do.

▶ *Be amazed that God will do what He called you to do!* (v. 24)

Choose to rely on His power to do what you are called to do.

KEY VERSE TO MEMORIZE

When you are walking through the valley of the shadow of depression, know God's heart and say out loud to yourself,

"I am still confident of this: I will see the goodness of the Lord in the land of the living."
(Psalm 27:13)

The Time Line Test for Masked Depression[25]

▶ *Draw* a long, horizontal line representing your life.

▶ *Divide* the line into three sections (childhood, youth, adulthood).

▶ *Denote* meaningful events, major changes, losses and hurts along the line, such as these:

- birth of siblings
- marriage
- change of school
- job loss/new job
- relocation
- illness
- death of loved ones or death of pets
- injury
- lost friendships
- financial loss
- broken engagement
- separation/divorce
- abuse
- retirement

▶ *Determine* whether there are significant losses and hurts you have not faced, such as these—

- divorce of parents

- false accusations
- abandonment
- unjust criticism
- rejection
- thwarted goals
- failures
- unrealized dreams

▶ **Discover** the source of your masked pain through earnest prayer.

PRAYER FOR DISCOVERY

*"Oh, Father, I come to You
as Your child for help. Calm my heart.
Enable me to see what I need to see.
Make me aware of my need for healing,
and show me Your truth.
Bring to my mind any hidden hurt
in my heart and the exact
circumstances that caused it.
Help me to allow You
to minister to my wounded heart.
I know You have the love and
the power to make me whole.
Thank You that I can have confidence
that You will perform
what You have promised.
In Your name, Amen."*

▶ *Define* the event in specific statements.

- "I am grieving over _____."

- "I was so embarrassed when___."

- "I felt abandoned by _____."

- "I was really hurt when _____."

- "I've been determined to never let _____ happen again."

▶ *Defuse* the power that the event has over your emotions by sharing it with a trusted person and with God.

▶ *Drop* the case you have against those who have hurt you, and forgive them as Christ forgave you.

> **"Bear with each other and forgive whatever grievances you may have against one another. Forgive as the Lord forgave you." (Colossians 3:13)**

Each person has a tangible body, an intangible soul and an intangible spirit and so is a "trichotomous" being. As a tri-part person, the following is true:

▶ Your *body* is your physical makeup (flesh, bones and blood).

▶ Your *soul* is your behavioral personality (mind, will, and emotions).

▶ Your human *spirit* is that innermost part of your being, which needs salvation, craves gratification of your deepest needs (for love, significance and security) and in the believer, the human spirit houses the Holy Spirit.

Medical professionals have known for years that how you choose to respond to life's inevitable tragedies and disappointments has consequences on your physical body. Depression, which can result from your mental and emotional state or from physical imbalances, will have profound effect on your spirit. God encourages us to seek healing and health in all three areas of life: body, soul, and spirit.

"May God himself, the God of peace, sanctify you through and through. May your whole spirit, soul and body be kept blameless at the coming of our Lord Jesus Christ." (1 Thessalonians 5:23)

47

Self-Directed Soul

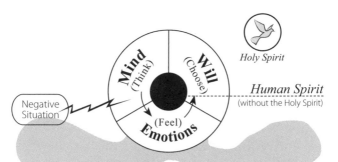

Your Self-Directed Reaction

Mind → Emotions → Will

Mind .... Your thinking.
Emotions .... Your feeling.
Will .... Your choosing to act.

Spirit-Directed Soul

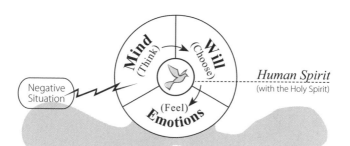

Your Spirit-Directed Response

Mind —→ Will —→ Emotions

Mind .... He teaches your mind.

Will .... He directs your will.

Emotions .... He controls your emotions.

The Physical Body

QUESTION: "Does taking medicine for depression show a lack of faith in God?"

ANSWER: Various physical problems can contribute to depression. For example, in bipolar, one of the major factors is a biochemical imbalance that is usually treated successfully with medication. Unfortunately, many Christians fear being labeled unspiritual if they seek medical help for their depression, yet by doing nothing they can suffer needlessly. Sometimes medication is needed for a period of time to "level out" mountainous swings so that those in the throes of depression can see truth and walk on level ground. Ezekiel 47:12 explains that God made *"leaves for healing."* Therefore, medicine is biblical.

However, medicine should be used, not to numb the pain or to escape it, but to help a person process the pain. Additionally, medication should be the last avenue—tried only after all other steps have been taken—and always in conjunction with counseling.

IF YOU ARE SUFFERING WITH PROLONGED DEPRESSION ...

▶First, obtain a thorough *medical checkup*. Tell the doctor you feel unusually depressed. Be specific.

▶Ask the doctor to evaluate all *medications* you are taking and eliminate what is unnecessary. Ask your doctor if any of your medications could contribute to depression.

▶Develop regular *sleeping habits—sleep is therapeutic*. Only during deep sleep does the brain produce serotonin, which alleviates depression. Set a regular time to go to sleep and to rise.

▶Maintain a *regular schedule* of activity.

▶Be actively involved in church functions and accept invitations to be with others—even if you don't feel like it.

▶*Eliminate stress*—avoid being overly fatigued.

▶Set aside some quiet time of relaxation.

▶Eat balanced, *nutritious meals* regularly.

▶Avoid caffeine, alcohol, salt and junk food. Stay away from sugar to avoid "the sugar blues."

▶Get *regular exercise*—walk, jog or swim at least four days a week. Twenty minutes of brisk walking releases endorphins—a natural mood elevator.

▶Spend *time in the sun* enjoying God's beautiful creation. Research reveals 30 minutes of sunshine can help alleviate depression.

WHAT IS SEASONAL AFFECTIVE DISORDER?

QUESTION: "Recently I moved to a town that has gloomy weather, and now I'm feeling gloomy. Everything else in my life is positive. What do I do? It's as if the fog outside my window has invaded my mind and muddled my thinking."

ANSWER: Seasonal Affective Disorder, or SAD, is a form of depression associated with deprivation of sunlight.[26] SAD, also called the "winter blues," typically begins in the fall with shorter days and less sunlight and subsides in the spring as the days get longer. Too little sunlight entering the eye produces in the brain a hormone called *melatonin*, which is released with the onset of darkness. Too much melatonin creates a biochemical imbalance in the hypothalamus region of the brain. In animals, melatonin controls hibernation and causes a decrease in activity. In humans, SAD causes symptoms such as excessive sleep, lethargy, overeating and depression.

The best treatment for SAD is light—light is therapeutic.

▶First, avail yourself of any and every opportunity to get into the natural sunlight (outdoor exercise, morning, noon or afternoon walks, or anytime the sun is shining).

▶Second, you could purchase a specially designed light box that produces artificial light and then expose yourself to the light for 30 minutes, or up to two hours daily.

▶Take vacations in places where you can soak in the sun.

> **"Light is sweet, and it pleases the eyes to see the sun." (Ecclesiastes 11:7)**

The Soul

When you have lost a significant relationship, whether by rejection, divorce, or death, it is normal for your heart to be depressed. However, after a period of time normal healing should have occurred. If your heart has not "resumed its natural shape," your heart could be in a *state of depression*. Since the entire soul (mind, will and emotions) is affected by depression, recovery involves taking steps to treat depression in all three areas of the soul. Each part that has been touched by depression needs to be reached with healing.

1 The Mind

What your mind dwells on can be a key ingredient to overcoming chronic depression. Research has verified that a person's thoughts literally change the chemistry of the brain. You need to fill your thinking with God's thinking—fill your mind with God's perspective and promises. Romans 12:2 says you are, *"transformed by the renewing of your mind."*

▶Write several Scriptures on index cards and read them several times a day.

▶Make a list, *My Thanksgiving List*, of seven good things in your life, and spend time every day thanking God for those things.

▶During the next week, list seven more specifics for which you can thank God.

▶Keep adding to the list each week.

By looking at God's Word you can discover God's purpose for allowing the painful losses in your life. Since God is a Redeemer, He has a purpose for allowing everything—even the storms in your life.

**"Finally, brothers, whatever is true, whatever is noble, whatever is right, whatever is pure, whatever is lovely, whatever is admirable—if anything is excellent or praiseworthy—think about such things."
(Philippians 4:8)**

BRING LIGHT INTO THE DARKNESS

In order to combat depression, first write out your dark thoughts. Then, as your rebuttal, write out what God says. Ask the Lord and a friend for help with wording. And then when dark thoughts come, use cognitive therapy on yourself, which simply means replacing your *dark thoughts of despair* with the *light of truth*.

**"You are my lamp, O LORD;
the LORD turns my darkness into light."
(2 Samuel 22:29)**

Darkness: "I cannot escape this darkness."

Light: "The Lord will bring light into my darkness."

"My God turns my darkness into light." (Psalm 18:28)

Darkness: "I feel like I have no refuge … no safe haven."

Light: "The Lord will be my refuge."

"Keep me safe, O God, for in you I take refuge." (Psalm 16:1)

Darkness: "I feel like I'm in too much trouble."

Light: "The Lord is my help in trouble."

"God is our refuge and strength, an ever-present help in trouble." (Psalm 46:1)

Darkness: "I can't help feeling so restless."

Light: "My God gives my soul rest."

"My soul finds rest in God alone; my salvation comes from him." (Psalm 62:1)

DARKNESS: "I can't see the path I should take."

LIGHT: "The Lord will direct my path."

"Trust in the Lord with all your heart and lean not on your own understanding; in all your ways acknowledge him, and he will make your paths straight." (Proverbs 3:5–6)

DARKNESS: "My burden is too heavy to bear."

LIGHT: "The Lord is my burden bearer."

"Praise be to the Lord, to God our Savior, who daily bears our burdens." (Psalm 68:19)

DARKNESS: "I'm afraid to be around people."

LIGHT: "The Lord will give me strength to be around people."

"The Lord is my light and my salvation— whom shall I fear? The Lord is the stronghold of my life—of whom shall I be afraid?" (Psalm 27:1)

DARKNESS: "My confidence is completely shaken."

LIGHT: "The Lord will keep my life from being shaken."

"I have set the Lord always before me. Because he is at my right hand, I will not be shaken." (Psalm 16:8)

2 The Will

People who have prolonged depression have a paralysis of the will and feel that life has stripped them of their choices. They feel stranded in the middle of the storm with no real options. But that is far from the truth. While it is true that life is sprinkled with unavoidable discouragement, you *can avoid* letting your mind become drenched with discouragement. That is your choice; it's an act of *the will*.

After an initial downpour, you can choose to stay in bed, procrastinate, and *rely on yourself* for relief, or you can choose to get underneath God's umbrella of protection and rely on Him. Jesus said, *"Do not let your hearts be troubled. Trust in God; trust also in me"* (John 14:1). You can choose to trust the Lord with your life; *He is worthy of your trust.* Even if you don't feel like it.

▶Listen to uplifting and inspirational music.

▶Keep your living environment bright and cheerful.

▶Maintain a clean, uncluttered environment.

▶Clear your home of objects associated with activities related to the demonic or the occult.

▶ Resist long periods of time on the telephone.

▶ Avoid spending too much time watching television.

▶ Write thank you and encouragement notes to others.

▶ Set small attainable goals every day.

▶ Look for something you can do for someone each day and you will experience God's truth that, indeed, *It is more blessed to give than to receive*" (Acts 20:35).

"My son, preserve sound judgment and discernment, do not let them out of your sight; they will be life for you, an ornament to grace your neck."
(Proverbs 3:21–22)

Biblical Example:

When King Saul needed soothing for his troubled soul, David played music on the lyre.

"Whenever the [evil] spirit from God came upon Saul, David would take his harp and play. Then relief would come to Saul; he would feel better, and the evil spirit would leave him."
(1 Samuel 16:23)

3 The Emotions

Often people who are depressed have difficulty expressing their feelings in a healthy way. A common cause of depression is buried feelings due to loss or past hurts. Ignored or denied feelings won't go away. They are buried alive, deep inside your soul, where they fester and create an infection that produces poison in your body. That is why it is vital to face your feelings.

Bring your heartache and hurts, your anxiety and anger, your fear and frustration to Jesus. Pour out your heart to Him and receive His comfort. He alone understands the depth of your pain. The Bible assures us,

**"We do not have a high priest
who is unable to sympathize
with our weaknesses, but we have one
who has been tempted in every way, just
as we are—yet was without sin. Let us
then approach the throne of grace with
confidence, so that we
may receive mercy and find grace
to help us in our time of need."
(Hebrews 4:15–16)**

QUESTION: "What is anniversary depression?"

ANSWER: Anniversary depression is a yearly recurring depression. This type of depression is an ***involuntary emotional reaction*** to past loss or trauma ...

▶ related to the anniversary date of a traumatic event

▶ lasting for a limited period of time with the onset triggered by memories

EXAMPLES:

▶ Following an abortion, many women dive into a depression each year around the anniversary of their child's abortion.

▶ Some spouses go into an anniversary depression around the date of their mate's death.

Ways to Deal with Anniversary Depression

▶ *Understand* that your depression is rooted in a real loss from your past. Realize that what you are experiencing is not uncommon.

▶ *Acknowledge* your emotions, write out all painful memories and process them with a helpful person you can trust.

▶ *Release* your pain to the Lord and receive His comfort and healing.

"Heal me, O Lord, and I will be healed;
save me and I will be saved,
for you are the one I praise."
(Jeremiah 17:14)

"Lord, You know the pain
I've felt over (list each hurt,
each failure and each person associated
with the pain—be specific).
I now release all this pain
into Your hands.
Set me free in my soul and spirit.
I'm so thankful You want to heal me
and to make me whole.
In Your precious name I pray.
Amen."

▶ *Anticipate* any upcoming anniversary and plan ahead for ways to counter possible depression. For instance, plan a trip with someone or arrange a social event so that you will not be alone and your mind will be focused on something other than the past event.

▶ *Turn* your anniversary date into an occasion that will produce new, positive memories by serving others in a meaningful way.

▶ *Realize* that harbored resentment blocks emotional health and can lead to bitterness of soul and even to physical problems. Let go of any thoughts of revenge or hatred toward anyone by releasing each offender, each offense and all the resulting pain to God. In so doing, you will be taking all that weight off your emotional hook and placing it on God's hook. He is faithful and just, and He will avenge you in His time and in His righteous way.

**"Be kind and compassionate
to one another,
forgiving each other, just as in
Christ God forgave you."
(Ephesians 4:32)**

The Spirit

The hope of every Christian is the indwelling Holy Spirit. *"'Not by might nor by power, but by my Spirit,' says the Lord Almighty."* (Zechariah 4:6)

Since He is literally God within us, it is through having Him that we actually have the mind of Christ and the sufficiency of Christ to meet every trial and overcome every difficulty. Even in the depths of your despair and the darkness of your depression, God is with you, for He is in you. When you cry in the night, He catches your tears and cradles your soul as a mother cradles her wailing infant and holds the child to her heart. Though you see Him not with your physical eyes, nor feel Him with your physical body, you can see Him with spiritual eyes and embrace Him with spiritual arms.

To overcome your depression, look inward, not to yourself, but to Him.

"His divine power has given us everything we need for life and godliness through our knowledge of him who called us by his own glory and goodness." (2 Peter 1:3)

LEARN TO CONQUER DEPRESSION

▶Confront any loss in your life, allowing yourself to grieve and be healed.

"[There is] a time to weep and a time to laugh, a time to mourn and a time to dance." (Ecclesiastes 3:4)

▶Offer your heart to God for cleansing, and confess your sins.

"If we claim to be without sin, we deceive ourselves and the truth is not in us. If we confess our sins, he is faithful and just and will forgive us our sins and purify us from all unrighteousness." (1 John 1:8–9)

▶Nurture thoughts that focus on God's great love for you.

"I have loved you with an everlasting love; I have drawn you with loving-kindness." (Jeremiah 31:3)

▶Quit negative thinking and negative self-talk.

"Finally, brothers, whatever is true, whatever is noble, whatever is right, whatever is pure, whatever is lovely, whatever is admirable—if anything is excellent or praiseworthy—think about such things." (Philippians 4:8)

▶ Understand God's eternal purpose for allowing personal loss and heartache.

"We know that in all things God works for the good of those who love him, who have been called according to his purpose." (Romans 8:28)

▶ Exchange your hurt and anger for the choice to give thanks (even when you don't feel thankful).

"Give thanks in all circumstances, for this is God's will for you in Christ Jesus." (1 Thessalonians 5:18)

▶ Remember that God is sovereign over your life, and He promises hope for your future.

"'I know the plans I have for you,' declares the Lord, 'plans to prosper you and not to harm you, plans to give you hope and a future.'" (Jeremiah 29:11)

God has a purpose for everything that touches you. Even the storm clouds in your life are useful in the hands of God. Depression can heighten your awareness of God and increase your dependency on God. It can open your eyes to His unique design for you before, during and after your bouts with despondency. Remember, just as storms replenish dry and parched ground and give birth to flowers and new life in the spring, so the storms in your life can revitalize your relationship with God and give birth to abundant fruit of the Spirit in your life.

> **"We know that in all things
> God works for the good of those
> who love him, who have been called
> according to his purpose."
> (Romans 8:28)**

▶ *Permitted by God* to warn you that something is wrong

"Before I was afflicted I went astray, but now I obey your word." (Psalm 119:67)

▶ *Permitted by God* to slow you down and cause you to reflect inwardly

"Therefore we do not lose heart. Though outwardly we are wasting away, yet

inwardly we are being renewed day by day."
(2 Corinthians 4:16)

▶ **Permitted by God** to reveal your weakness

"[The Lord said] 'My grace is sufficient for you, for my power is made perfect in weakness.' Therefore I will boast all the more gladly about my weaknesses, so that Christ's power may rest on me." (2 Corinthians 12:9)

▶ **Permitted by God** to bring you to Himself

"Let us draw near to God with a sincere heart in full assurance of faith, having our hearts sprinkled to cleanse us from a guilty conscience and having our bodies washed with pure water." (Hebrews 10:22)

▶ **Permitted by God** to develop your trust in Him

"Why are you downcast, O my soul? Why so disturbed within me? Put your hope in God, for I will yet praise him, my Savior and my God." (Psalm 43:5)

▶ **Permitted by God** to increase your compassion and understanding for others

"The Father of compassion and the God of all comfort ... comforts us in all our troubles, so that we can comfort those in any trouble with the comfort we ourselves have received from God." (2 Corinthians 1:3–4)

▶ *Permitted by God* to develop perseverance and maturity

"Consider it pure joy … whenever you face trials of many kinds, because you know that the testing of your faith develops perseverance. Perseverance must finish its work so that you may be mature and complete, not lacking anything." (James 1:2–4)

▶ *Permitted by God* to develop worth and value in your life

"Are not five sparrows sold for two pennies? Yet not one of them is forgotten by God. Indeed, the very hairs of your head are all numbered. Don't be afraid; you are worth more than many sparrows." (Luke 12:6–7)

▶ *Permitted by God* to cause you to rely on His resources

"His divine power has given us everything we need for life and godliness through our knowledge of him who called us by his own glory and goodness. Through these he has given us his very great and precious promises, so that through them you may participate in the divine nature and escape the corruption in the world caused by evil desires." (2 Peter 1:3–4)

▶ *Permitted by God* to be a healing process for damaged emotions

"Heal me, O Lord, and I will be healed; save me and I will be saved, for you are the one I praise." (Jeremiah 17:14)

A Positive Perspective on Depression

The famous English pastor Charles Haddon Spurgeon (often referred to as the greatest preacher of the nineteenth century) openly described his own depression, and with his very description, we gain much insight.

The times most favourable to fits of depression, so far as I have experienced, may be summed up in a brief catalogue. First among them I must mention *the hour of a great success*. When at last a long-cherished desire is fulfilled, when God has been glorified greatly by our means, and a great triumph achieved, then we are apt to faint.

Before any great achievement, some measure of the same depression is very usual. Surveying the difficulties before us, our hearts sink within us. This depression comes over me whenever the Lord is preparing a larger blessing for my ministry.

In the midst of a long stretch of unbroken labor, the same affliction may be looked for. The bow cannot be always bent without fear of breaking. Repose is as needful to the mind as sleep to the body.

This evil will also come upon us, we know not why, and then it is all the more difficult to drive it away. Causeless depression is not to be reasoned with. If those who laugh at such melancholy did but feel the grief of it for one hour, their laughter would be sobered into compassion.

If it be enquired why the Valley of the Shadow of Death must so often be traversed by the servants of King Jesus, the answer is not far to find. All this is promotive of the Lord's mode of working, which is summed up in these words: "*Not by might nor by power, but by my Spirit, saith the Lord.*" Heaven shall be all the fuller of bliss because we have been filled with anguish here below, and earth shall be better tilled because of our training in the school of adversity.[27]

When your heart is pressed down to the ground and living life makes you feel depressed, allow your depression to press you closer to the Lord, let Him lead you into the light.

**"We are hard pressed on every side,
but not crushed; perplexed,
but not in despair; persecuted,
but not abandoned; struck down,
but not destroyed."
(2 Corinthians 4:8–9)**

How to Find Hope When Hope Seems Elusive

When you are weary, when life isn't worth living, when hope seems elusive, what do you need to know? You need to know your Burden-Bearer—you need to know Jesus. He wants to be the Shepherd of your soul. His compassionate comfort extends to all those who have lost all hope. He says,

**"Come to me,
all you who are weary and burdened,
and I will give you rest."
(Matthew 11:28)**

When you are weary, how do you receive this rest within your soul? Allow these four truths to set you free.

Four Points of God's Plan

#1 God's Purpose for You is *Salvation*.

What was God's motivation in sending Christ to earth?

To express His love for you by saving you! The Bible says, *"God so loved the world that he gave his one and only Son, that whoever believes in him shall not perish but have eternal life. For God did not send his Son into the world to condemn the world, but to save the world through him."* (John 3:16–17)

What was Jesus' purpose in coming to earth?

To forgive your sins, to empower you to have victory over sin, and to enable you to live a fulfilled life! Jesus said, *"I have come that they may have life, and have it more abundantly."* (John 10:10 NKJV)

#2 Your Problem is *Sin*.

What exactly is sin?

Sin is living independently of God's standard—knowing what is right, but choosing what is wrong. The Bible says, *"Anyone, then, who knows the good he ought to do and doesn't do it, sins."* (James 4:17)

What is the major consequence of sin?

Spiritual death, eternal separation from God. Scripture states, *"Your iniquities [sins] have separated you from your God. The wages of sin is death, but the gift of God is eternal life in Christ Jesus our Lord."* (Isaiah 59:2; Romans 6:23)

#3 God's Provision for You is the *Savior.*

Can anything remove the penalty for sin?

Yes! Jesus died on the cross to personally pay the penalty for your sins. The Bible says, *"God demonstrates his own love for us in this: While we were still sinners, Christ died for us"* (Romans 5:8).

What is the solution to being separated from God?

Belief in (entrusting your life to) Jesus Christ as the only way to God the Father. Jesus says, "I am the way and the truth and the life. No one comes to the Father except through me." (John 14:6) *"Believe in the Lord Jesus, and you will be saved."* (Acts 16:31)

#4 Your Part is *Surrender.*

Give Christ control of your life, entrusting yourself to Him. *"Jesus said to his disciples, 'If anyone would come after me, he must deny himself and take up his cross [die to your own self-rule] and follow me. For whoever wants to save his life will lose it, but whoever loses his life for me will find it. What good will it be for a man if he gains the whole world, yet forfeits his soul?'"* (Matthew 16:24–26)

Place your faith in (rely on) Jesus Christ as your personal Lord and Savior and reject your "good works" as a means of earning God's approval. *"It is by grace you have been saved, through faith—and this not from yourselves, it is the gift of God—not by works, so that no one can boast."* (Ephesians 2:8–9)

The moment you choose to receive Jesus as your Lord and Savior—entrusting your life to Him—He comes to live inside you. Then He gives you His power to live the fulfilled life God has planned for you.

If you want to be fully forgiven by God and become the person God created you to be, you can tell Him in a simple, heartfelt prayer like this:

PRAYER OF SALVATION

"God, I want a real relationship with
You. I admit that many times
I've chosen to go my own way
instead of Your way.
Please forgive me for my sins.
Jesus, thank You for dying on the cross
to pay the penalty for my sins.
Come into my life to be
my Lord and my Savior.
Change me from the inside out
and make me the person
You created me to be.
In Your holy name I pray.
Amen."

What Can You Expect Now?

If you sincerely prayed this prayer, look at what God says!

"In his great mercy he has given us new birth into a living hope."
(1 Peter 1:3)

▶ ***Don't say:*** "You shouldn't feel that way."

Say: "I care about what you are feeling."

- Ask, "Would you like to share your feelings with me?"

- Say, "If ever you want to talk, I'm here for you."

"The purposes of a man's heart are deep waters, but a man of understanding draws them out." (Proverbs 20:5)

▶ ***Don't say:*** "You must eat! Think of all the starving children in Africa."

Say: "Even if we're not hungry, we both need to eat. A car needs gas for energy—we both need food for energy."

- Bring nutritious food to their home.

- Take them out to eat or perhaps on a picnic.

- Encourage healthy eating habits. (No junk food, no sugar—sugar gives a temporary high, then the blood sugar drops, creating the "sugar blues.")

The Bible says we need *"Food for the stomach."* (1 Corinthians 6:13)

▶ ***Don't say:*** "You need to quit taking that medicine."

Say: "Not all medicines work the same for everyone. I'll go with you to get a thorough medical evaluation so that the doctor will make sure the medicine is working for you."

- Talk specifically to a competent doctor who specializes in depression.

- Don't be afraid to get a second opinion.

"Plans fail for lack of counsel, but with many advisers they succeed." (Proverbs 15:22)

▶ ***Don't say:*** "You just need to pray more."

Say: "I'm praying for you, and I'm going to keep praying."

- Pray with them, and tell them you are praying for them.

- Ask specifically, "How can I pray for you today?"

"Far be it from me that I should sin against the Lord by failing to pray for you." (1 Samuel 12:23)

▶ ***Don't say:*** "You just need to read the Bible more!"

Say: "There are several passages in the Bible that have given me much hope, and

I've written them out for you. May I share them with you?"

- Give them hope-filled Scriptures to read three times a day: after awakening, midday and bedtime. (Jeremiah 29:11; Psalm 130:5)

- Help them memorize Scripture. (Philippians 4:6–8; 4:13; 4:19)

"I rise before dawn and cry for help; I have put my hope in your word." (Psalm 119:147)

▶ ***Don't say:*** "You need to get involved in a church."

Say: "I'm involved in a church where I've been learning how meaningful life can be. I would love for you to come with me next Sunday, and afterward we can have lunch together."

- Invite them to come to church with you.

- Involve them in a small group Bible study.

"Let us not give up meeting together, as some are in the habit of doing, but let us encourage one another." (Hebrews 10:25)

▶ ***Don't say:*** "Snap out of it! Get over it!"

Say: "I'm going to stick with you, and we'll get through this together."

- Admit, "I don't know everything I wish I knew, but I'm willing to help."

- State, "If you can't hold on to God, hold on to me because I'm holding on to God."

"There is a friend who sticks closer than a brother." (Proverbs 18:24)

HOW YOU Can Help

When you have depressed loved ones in your life, you want to do something that will make a difference, but the question is *what?* Most important of all is *do not avoid them.*

Find ways to show you care, such as, plan a fun activity with them, read to them, exercise with them (walk, jog, swim). Invite them to outside events or even to run errands with you. Because of their tendency to withdraw and isolate, help them get *involved* in activities—not just as a spectator; perhaps, help them find a hobby. Just realize, you may be their only *lifeline of hope*—and *they need to stay "connected."* Do what you wish someone else would do for you if you were the one struggling with depression.

"Do to others as you would have them do to you."
(Luke 6:31)

▶ Learn all you can about depression—read books, watch videos, attend seminars.

"Apply your heart to instruction and your ears to words of knowledge." (Proverbs 23:12)

▶ If suicide is a concern, ask, "Are you thinking about hurting yourself/taking your life?" They may get mad, but it's better to have a *mad* friend than a *dead* friend.

"The tongue has the power of life and death." (Proverbs 18:21)

▶ Take all threats of suicide and self-injury seriously—15 percent of those who are depressed ultimately kill themselves.[28]

"The words of a man's mouth are deep waters." (Proverbs 18:4)

▶ Be an accountability partner—"I'm with you in this, and I won't abandon you."

"Two are better than one, because they have a good return for their work." (Ecclesiastes 4:9)

▶ Initiate dialogue regularly—frequent phone calls, intentional contact.

"The wise in heart are called discerning, and pleasant words promote instruction." (Proverbs 16:21)

▶ Listen to them and hear their pain—listening affirms their value.

"Everyone should be quick to listen, slow to speak and slow to become angry." (James 1:19)

▶ Talk about depression—talking helps remove the stigma of depression.

"A word aptly spoken is like apples of gold in settings of silver." (Proverbs 25:11)

▶ Verbally encourage them—sincerely and often.

"Encourage one another and build each other up." (1 Thessalonians 5:11)

▶ Realize the power of touch—a hand on the shoulder and appropriate hugs and kisses.

"Greet one another with a kiss of love." (1 Peter 5:14)

▶ Give them inspirational praise music to lift their spirits—music is therapeutic.

"Speak to one another with psalms, hymns and spiritual songs." (Ephesians 5:19)

▶ Bring laughter into their lives—fun cards, videos, movies and people.

"A cheerful heart is good medicine." (Proverbs 17:22)

▶ Give them "nutritional therapy"—for example, vitamins B-6 and E, calcium, magnesium and folic acid are helpful for combating depression. Ask your doctor.

God made *"leaves for healing."*
(Ezekiel 47:12)

▶ Help them set small daily goals that require minimum effort—check on their progress regularly.

"The desires of the diligent are fully satisfied."
(Proverbs 13:4)

▶ Enlist help from other family and friends— be specific about your concerns.

"Carry each other's burdens, and in this way you will fulfill the law of Christ."
(Galatians 6:2)

You may ask, "How could a good and loving God allow such a tragedy to these five young children?" We may never understand it all, but we can know …

"Though he brings grief, he will show compassion, so great is his unfailing love. For he does not willingly bring affliction or grief to the children of men."
(Lamentations 3:32–33)

SCRIPTURES TO MEMORIZE

When I am depressed, in what can **I put my hope**?

"I wait for the Lord, my soul waits, and in his word I put my hope." (Psalm 130:5)

When I am depressed, **who** will **sustain me**?

*"Surely God is my help; the LORD is the one **who sustains me**."* (Psalm 54:4)

When I am depressed, what should I **think about**?

*"Whatever is true, whatever is noble, whatever is right, whatever is pure, whatever is lovely, whatever is admirable— if anything is excellent or praiseworthy— **think about** such things."* (Philippians 4:8)

When I am depressed, what will **guard my heart and mind**?

*"In everything, by prayer and petition, with thanksgiving, present your requests to God. And the peace of God, which transcends all understanding, will **guard** your **hearts** and your **minds** in Christ Jesus."* (Philippians 4:6–7)

When I feel depressed, what will motivate me to **persevere under this trial**?

> *"Blessed is the man who **perseveres under trial**, because when he has stood the test, he will receive the crown of life that God has promised to those who love him."* (James 1:12)

When I feel **downcast** and **my soul** is **disturbed within me**, what can I do?

> *"Why are you **downcast**, O **my soul**? Why so **disturbed within me**? Put your hope in God, for I will yet praise him, my Savior and my God."* (Psalm 42:11)

When I am depressed, should I get **counsel** from numerous advisors?

> *"Plans fail for lack of **counsel**, but with many advisers they succeed."* (Proverbs 15:22)

When I get into **waters** of deep depression, will I get **through** it?

> *"When you pass **through the waters**, I will be with you; and when you pass through the rivers, they will not sweep over you. When you walk through the fire, you will not be burned; the flames will not set you ablaze."* (Isaiah 43:2)

When I feel depressed with **unrelenting pain**, can I find any joy or consolation?

*"I would still have this consolation—my joy in **unrelenting pain**—that I had not denied the words of the Holy One."*
(Job 6:10)

When I've lost all **hope** for the **future**, does God have any **plans** for me?

*"'For I know the **plans** I have for you,' declares the LORD, '**plans** to prosper you and not to harm you, **plans** to give you **hope** and a **future**.'"* (Jeremiah 29:11)

NOTES

1. *"Texas mother charged with killing her 5 children."* June 21, 2001, http://www.cnn.com/2001/US/06/20/children.killed/index.html.

2. Archibald D. Hart, "The Psychopathology of Postpartum Disorders," *Christian Counseling Today* 10, no. 4 (2002): 16–17.

3. *Merriam-Webster's Collegiate Dictionary* (electronic edition) (Merriam-Webster, 2001).

4. *Merriam-Webster's Collegiate Dictionary.*

5. James Strong, *Strong's Greek Lexicon* (electronic edition; Online Bible Millennium Edition v. 1.13) (Timnathserah Inc., July 6, 2002).

6. H. Norman Wright, *Beating the Blues: Overcoming Depression and Stress* (Ventura, CA: Regal, 1988), 9.

7. *Merriam-Webster's Collegiate Dictionary.*

8. *Merriam-Webster's Collegiate Dictionary.*

9. Stephen A. Grunlan and Daniel H. Lambrides, *Healing Relationships: A Christian's Manual for Lay Counseling* (Camp Hill, PA: Christian Publications, 1984), 121.

10. A *disorder* means that a person's normal functioning of life is impaired. A person with a *depressive disorder* has "clinical depression."

11. A *disorder* means that a person's normal functioning of life is impaired. A person with a *depressive disorder* has "clinical depression."

12. American Psychiatric Association, *Diagnostic and Statistical Manual of Mental Disorders*, 4th ed., text revision (Washington, DC: American Psychiatric Association, 2000), 345, 403–5.

13. *Merriam-Webster's Collegiate Dictionary.*

14. Archibald D. Hart, *Counseling the Depressed*, vol. 5, Resources for Christian Counseling, ed. Gary R. Collins (Dallas: Word, 1987), 34.

15. Christy Oglesby, "Postpartum depression: More than 'baby blues.'" June 27, 2001, http://www.cnn.com/2001/HEALTH/parenting/06/26/postpartum.depression/index.html; DSM-IV TR, 422–23; Archibald Hart, and Catherine Hart Weber, *Unveiling Depression in Women: A Practical Guide to Understanding and Overcoming Depression* (Grand Rapids: Fleming H. Revell, 2002), 126.

16. Timothy Roche, "Andrea Yates: More to the Story." March 18, 2002, http://www.time.com/time/nation/article/0,8599,218445,00.html.

17. DSM-IV TR, 422–3; Michael R. Lyles, "Psychiatric Aspects of Postpartum Mood Disorders," *Christian Counseling Today* 10, no. 4 (2002): 19.

18. DSM-IV TR, 422.

19. Hart and Weber, *Unveiling Depression in Women*, 56.

20. Hart and Weber, *Unveiling Depression in Women*, 55.

21. Michael Lyles, *Women and Depression*, Extraordinary Women, EW 301, VHS (Forest, VA: American Association of Christian Counselors, n.d.).

22. James W. Jefferson, "My Hippocampus Is Bigger than Yours!" *Geriatric Times* 1, no. 4 (2000), http://www.geriatrictimes.com/g001220.html.

23. *Merriam-Webster's Collegiate Dictionary.*

24. *The Andrea Yates Story*, VHS (A & E Television Networks, 2003).

25. Charlotte A. Greeson, Mary Hollingsworth, and Michael Washburn, *The Grief Adjustment Guide: A Pathway Through Pain*, Faire & Hale Planner (Sisters, OR: Questar, 1990), 200–202.

26. Hart and Weber, *Unveiling Depression in Women*, 180–81; "Symptoms." SADAssociation, http://www.sada.org.uk/symptoms.htm.

27. Charles H. Spurgeon, *Lectures to My Students*, new ed., Ministry Resources Library (Grand Rapids: Zondervan, 1980), 158–64.

28. Roy W. Fairchild, "Sadness and Depression," in *Dictionary of Pastoral Care and Counseling*, ed. Rodney J. Hunter, et al. (Nashville: Abingdon, 1990), 1103–6.

SELECTED BIBLIOGRAPHY

The Andrea Yates Story. VHS. n.p.: A & E Television Networks, 2003.

American Psychiatric Association. *Diagnostic and Statistical Manual of Mental Disorders*. 4th ed., text revision. Washington, DC: American Psychiatric Association, 2000.

Carlson, Dwight L. *Why Do Christians Shoot Their Wounded? Helping (Not Hurting) Those with Emotional Difficulties*. Downers Grove, IL: InterVarsity, 1994.

Fairchild, Roy W. "Sadness and Depression." In *Dictionary of Pastoral Care and Counseling*, edited by Rodney J. Hunter, et al., 1103-Nashville: Abingdon, 1990.

Greeson, Charlotte A., Mary Hollingsworth, and Michael Washburn. *The Grief Adjustment Guide: A Pathway Through Pain*. Faire & Hale Planner. Sisters, OR: Questar, 1990.

Grunlan, Stephen A., and Daniel H. Lambrides. *Healing Relationships: A Christian's Manual for Lay Counseling*. Camp Hill, PA: Christian Publications, 1984.

Hart, Archibald D. "The Psychopathology of Postpartum Disorders." *Christian Counseling Today* 10, no. 4 (2002): 16–17.

Hart, Archibald D. *Coping with Depression in the Ministry and Other Helping Professions*. Dallas: Word, 1984.

Hart, Archibald D. *Counseling the Depressed.* Resources for Christian Counseling, ed. Gary R. Collins, vol. Dallas: Word, 1987.

Hart, Archibald D. *Dark Clouds, Silver Linings.* Colorado Springs, CO: Focus on the Family, 1993.

Hart, Archibald, and Catherine Hart Weber. *Unveiling Depression in Women: A Practical Guide to Understanding and Overcoming Depression.* Grand Rapids: Fleming H. Revell, 2002.

Jefferson, James W. "My Hippocampus Is Bigger than Yours!" *Geriatric Times* 1, no. 4 (2000), http://www.geriatrictimes.com/g001220.html.

Lyles, Michael R. "Psychiatric Aspects of Postpartum Mood Disorders." *Christian Counseling Today* 10, no. 4 (2002): 18–20.

Lyles, Michael R. *Women and Depression,* Extraordinary Women, EW 3VHS. Forest, VA: American Association of Christian Counselors, n.d.

Minirth, Frank B., and Paul D. Meier. *Happiness Is a Choice: The Symptoms, Causes, and Cures of Depression.* 2nd ed. Grand Rapids: Baker, 1994.

Oglesby, Christy. "Postpartum depression: More than 'baby blues.'" June 27, 2001, http://www.cnn.com/2001/HEALTH/parenting/06/26/postpartum.depression/index.html.

Roche, Timothy. "Andrea Yates: More to the Story." March 18, 2002, http://www.time.com/time/nation/article/0,8599,218445,00.html.

Spotts, Steven W. *Depression*. A Rapha Recovery Booklet. Dallas: Word, 1991.

Spurgeon, Charles H. *Lectures to My Students*. New ed. Ministry Resources Library. Grand Rapids: Zondervan, 1980.

"Symptoms." SADAssociation, http://www.sada.org.uk/symptoms.htm.

"Texas mother charged with killing her 5 children." June 21, 2001, http://www.cnn.com/2001/US/06/20/children.killed/index.html.

Wright, H. Norman. *Beating the Blues: Overcoming Depression and Stress*. Ventura, CA: Regal, 1988.

HOPE FOR THE HEART TITLES

The HOPE FOR THE HEART Biblical Counseling Library is Your Solution!

- Easy-to-read, perfect for anyone.
- Short. Only 96 pages. Good for the busy person.
- Christ-centered biblical advice and practical help
- Tested and proven over 20 years of June Hunt's radio ministry
- 30 titles in the series – each tackling a key issue people face today.
- Affordable. You or your church can give away, lend, or sell them.

Display available for churches and ministries.

www.hendricksonrose.com